**PRO** SPORTS
**SUPERSTARS**

# Superstars
## of the
# NEW YORK
# GIANTS

by Matt Scheff

AMICUS HIGH INTEREST 🦴 AMICUS INK

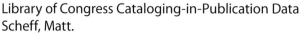

Amicus High Interest and
Amicus Ink are imprints of Amicus
P.O. Box 1329, Mankato, MN 56002
www.amicuspublishing.us

Library of Congress Cataloging-in-Publication Data
Scheff, Matt.
  Superstars of the New York Giants / Matt Scheff.
     pages  cm. -- (Pro sports superstars)
  Includes index.
  ISBN 978-1-60753-528-7 (hardcover) -- ISBN 978-1-60753-558-4 (eBook)
  ISBN 978-1-68152-065-0 (paperback)
  1.  New York Giants (Football team)--History--Juvenile literature.
  2.  Football players--New York (State)--Juvenile literature.  I. Title.
  GV956.N4S34 2014
  796.332'64097471--dc23
                              2013010600

Photo Credits: David Drapkin/AP Images, cover, 5; Bill Kostroun/AP
Images, 2, 18; AP Images, 6, 9, 10; NFL Photos/AP Images, 13; Paul Spinelli/
NFL Photos/AP Images, 14, 22; Kathy Willens/AP Images, 17; George
Widman/AP Images, 21

Produced for Amicus by The Peterson Publishing Company
and Red Line Editorial.

Editor:  Jenna Gleisner
Designer:  Becky Daum


Printed in Mankato, MN

HC  10  9  8  7  6  5  4
PB  10  9  8  7  6  5  4  3  2

# TABLE OF CONTENTS

# MEET THE NEW YORK GIANTS

The New York Giants joined the **NFL** in 1925. They have won eight **titles**. Four of them were Super Bowls. The Giants have had many stars. Here are some of the best.

# EMLEN TUNNELL

Emlen Tunnell **intercepted** many passes. He was also great at returning kicks. He was very fast. Tunnell won an NFL title in 1956.

Tunnell was the first African American player elected to the Pro Football Hall of Fame.

# FRANK GIFFORD

Frank Gifford could do it all. He was a great runner. He could also catch and pass. He even kicked. Gifford was the NFL **MVP** in 1956.

Gifford went to the Pro Bowl at three different positions.

# ROSEY BROWN

Rosey Brown was strong and quick. He was a great blocker. Brown played 13 seasons for the Giants. He helped them win the NFL title in 1956. He also went to nine Pro Bowls.

# HARRY CARSON

Harry Carson was a star on **defense**. He always played hard. He was best at stopping the run. Carson helped the Giants win the 1986 Super Bowl.

# LAWRENCE TAYLOR

Lawrence Taylor was one of the best players ever. He was a great tackler. He got a lot of **sacks**. Taylor was the MVP in 1986. He helped the Giants win two Super Bowls.

# MICHAEL STRAHAN

Michael Strahan loved to get sacks. He has more than any other Giants player. Strahan won a Super Bowl with the Giants. He went to seven Pro Bowls.

Strahan's best season was 2001. He set the record for sacks that year.

# TIKI BARBER

Tiki Barber was quick and smart. He was also good at catching the ball. He is the Giants' leader in **rushing** yards.

Barber played in three Pro Bowls in a row starting in 2004.

# ELI MANNING

Eli Manning plays his best in big games. He led the Giants to the 2007 and 2011 Super Bowls. They won both of them. Manning was the Super Bowl MVP both times.

The Giants have had some great players. Who will be the next star?

# TEAM FAST FACTS

**Founded:** 1925

**Nicknames:** The G-Men, Big Blue

**Home Stadium:** MetLife Stadium (East Rutherford, New Jersey)

**Super Bowl Titles:** 4 (1986, 1990, 2007, and 2011)

**Hall of Fame Players:** 18, including Emlen Tunnell, Frank Gifford, Rosey Brown, Harry Carson, and Lawrence Taylor

# WORDS TO KNOW

**defense** – the group of players that tries to stop the other team from scoring

**intercept** – when a defensive player catches a pass

**MVP** – Most Valuable Player; an honor given to the best player each season

**NFL** – National Football League; the league pro football players play in

**Pro Bowl** – the NFL's all-star game

**rushing** – running with the ball

**sack** – a tackle of the quarterback on a passing play

**title** – a championship

# LEARN MORE

## Books

Goodman, Michael E. *The Story of the New York Giants*. Mankato, MN: Creative Education, 2010.

MacRae, Sloan. *The New York Giants*. New York: Powerkids Press, 2011.

## Web Sites

### New York Giants—Official Site
http://www.giants.com
Watch video clips and view photos of the New York Giants

### NFL.com
http://nfl.com
Check out pictures and your favorite football players' stats.

### NFL Rush
http://www.nflrush.com
Play games and learn how to be a part of NFL PLAY 60.

# INDEX